WHEN THE JURY
MONEY
VOTE
AND PRIDE COMES
BLACK

A Strategy For Power & Justice In Black America

By

ZULU ALI, ESQ.

TABLE OF CONTENTS

DEDICATION

Dedicated to My Beautiful and Loving Mother:
LINDA JEAN REESE HARVEY

ABOUT THE AUTHOR

Zulu Ali is a practicing trial attorney, businessman, social commentator, and activist. A former police officer and U.S. Marine Corps veteran, he earned a doctorate in law (J.D.) from Trinity International University; master's in the administration of Justice (M.S.) and business (M.B.A.) from the University of Phoenix; an undergraduate degree with a focus on African Studies from Regents College through a consortium with Tennessee State University; and police officer certification (P.O.S.T.) from the Tennessee Law Enforcement Training Academy.

He is a postgraduate scholar of international and treaty law at Euclid University, West Africa, and a doctoral scholar of business with a research focus on Pan-African business and trade at California Southern University.

Attorney Ali is the founder and principal attorney at the Law Offices of Zulu Ali and Associates, LLP, based in Riverside, California, where he focuses on representing persons accused of crimes, immigrants, and persons seeking civil justice in state and federal courts. Ali is also admitted to represent persons at the African Court of Justice and Human Rights in Tanzania and the International Criminal Court at The Hague, Netherlands.

Attorney Ali and his law firm takes on complicated cases and matters that provided an opportunity to make changes in the law, through the courts, when the law is unjust. Attorney Ali served as Director of the American Committee for United Nations Oversight, an advocacy group that lobbied the United Nations for police reform in 2015. He is the Director of the Stop and Frisk Academy, which mentors and trains at-risk youth to deal with police encounters; Director of the Southern California Veterans Legal Clinic, a legal clinic offering no-cost and low-cost legal services to military veterans; and a member of the National Conference of Black Lawyers.

In 2020, Attorney Ali was inducted as biographee in the MarquisWho's Who in America for excellence in law and activism. In 2017, Attorney Ali was recognized as one of the most influential African American Leaders in Los Angeles by the National Action Network founded by Reverend Al Sharpton. Attorney Ali has been Honored as a Top Lawyer by the National Black Lawyers-Top 100 and National Trial Lawyers-Top 100; a Top 10 Lawyer by the American Academy of Trial Attorneys, American Institute of Legal Counsel, American Jurist Institute, and Attorney & Practice Magazine; Litigator of the Year by the American Institute of Trial Lawyers; and Rue Ratings Best Lawyer in America.

He is the founder and CEO of 10 Nubian Queens & 5 Kings Media, a mass media production company focusing on black family and social justice content in film, radio, theatre, music, and book publishing. Ali produced the documentary film *Purpose & Freedom: Keep Your Hand on the Plow*, which premiered at the Wilshire Screening Room in Beverly Hills in 2017 and on-demand; wrote and produced the stage play *Purpose & Freedom: The Story of Attorney Zulu Ali & Aracely Morales*, which premiered at the Hudson Theater in Hollywood in January 2020; and wrote and produced a musical compilation with various artists titled *The Discography of Zulu Ali.*

Attorney Ali authored the books *Lecture on Black America and American Justice: A History & Paradigm of Retributive Psychosis* (2016);

and *Blackman's Religion: Islam or Christianity* (1997), a copy of which is in the Collection of Rosa Parks Papers at the Library of Congress.

Additionally, Zulu Ali hosts the nationally syndicated radio talk show *Justice Watch with Attorney Zulu Ali*, which broadcasts from an NBC Radio studio in Redlands, California, and he is a member of the National Black Radio Hall of Fame (Chicago chapter).

Ali has been married to his wife (Charito) since 1986, has four adult children, three grandchildren, and resides in Southern California with his family. Born and raised in central Tennessee by a single mother, Linda Reese Harvey, who Ali considers his hero; he is the grandson of the late A.D. and Bessie Reynolds; Perry and Catherine Reese; and Mr and Ms Edward Castleman.

As a youth, Ali attended Tennessee public schools, where he participated and lettered in varsity football. He is a descendant of Africans of Ibo and Balante distinction brought to central Tennessee in the eighteenth century (1700s) and subjected to forced subjugation. His family has resided in the central Tennessee area since the eighteenth century and, despite forced subjugation, has contributed significantly to national wealth, community service, military service, and a variety of professional fields.

INTRODUCTION

When the Jury, Money, Vote, and Pride Comes Black addresses the four critical elements of justice and equality for African Americans. Justice and balance will be realized with black jury participation and inclusion, economic power through ownership, voting collectively, and commitment to black history, culture, and values (pride).

For purposes of this book, the word white and white racist will apply to persons of European descent who subscribe to hatred and ignorance towards other people based on their inferiority and sickness. The term superiority will apply to persons of European descent who are fearful of different ethnic groups due to retribution and extinction.

Black and African Americans will be used interchangeably as a reference or description of the African inhabitants (and descendants) who were kidnapped, raped, and transported as chattel to North America and other places, and used as chattel to enrich the European colonists and prisoners who came to North America.

Racial discrimination has become a natural phenomenon in the world at large. The consequences of this discrimination are that individuals are described using colour and race as a distinguishing factor.

Racial discrimination, as it relates to white racist, is primarily fueled by greed and fear. The desire for more than a rational share of resources, selfishness, and fear of being treated inhumanely by those who white racist have tortured, brutalized, and murdered; and fear of extinction as those with melanin dominate genetically is the foundation of racial discrimination.

Since African Americans came to North America, there have been centuries of conditioning, where they were subjugated to being animals. The U.S. Supreme Court, in the case of *Dred Scott*, determined that black people were not human beings. The centuries of mental and physical torture imposed on black people is unprecedented, and the worst human rights crime imposed against people in the history of the world. The only shining light is that black people rose above this inhumane treatment and are the foundation of one of the most powerful nations in human history.

However, in light of black people building this nation, white racist continues to perpetuate its inhumane acts based on the continuing fear of losing resources, retribution, and extinction.

During the civil rights era, black people thought integration would result in equality, however, this belief has proved untrue and misguided.

Black people have tried to integrate into American society to be seen strictly as human beings and enjoy the fruits of their ancestors' labour without being subjected to institutional and systematic injustice in the areas of the economy, law, and politics.

Without a collective strategy to address the economic, legal, and political issues negatively impacting the black community, justice and power will be a dream and nightmare.

The times are long gone when the black community can depend on white people as a means of survival; if any such time ever existed. The most powerful human emotion is fear. The white racists fear what the black community would do if society flipped. Superiority is not the catalyst of acts perpetrated by a white racist. Today we see those who support the white racist paradigm openly advocated by President

Donald Trump; it is pure FEAR. The culture and survival of white racists standard is in danger of extinction, more than ever before, and they will fight to keep it.

Now that it is clear that the propelling force behind the attitudes of whites against the black community is fear, it is critical and necessary to take action to change the focus. Rather than lean on other people for support, African Americans must devise and focus on strategies to help them solve these issues themselves.

Black people must participate in the jury process; engage in group economics; voting collectively; and be committed to black history, culture, and values (pride). Without a doubt, if the community focuses on these four elements, they will enjoy power and justice.

This book is an enlightening piece that discusses the unpleasant situations and circumstances that African Americans are plagued within American society. While it addresses the injustice meted out to the black community as a result of the color of skin, it also provides solutions to ensure that African Americans are no longer treated as second-class citizens.

CHAPTER ONE

WHEN WE COME BLACK

People who live in the continents of Africa and Asia makeup the vast majority of the people in the world. There could never be a perception of the dominance of Europeans without spreading the pseudo concept of skin color. There are black, brown, and white (albinos) indigenous Africans born on the continent of Africa; and there are black, brown, and white indigenous Asians born on the continent of Asia. The word aborigines is used to describe the original people of the land, and, in all cases, aborigines are dark-skinned people.

Tribalism has existed since the beginning of time. People of different tribes and nations have mistreated each other, fought against, and enslaved each other. It is all inhumane and generally unjustified. The traditional notion of slavery in the Torah, Bible, Quran, and societies that practised the institution; usually did not practice it in the manner in which the Europeans did during the transatlantic slave trade. Human beings doing labour for another person or entity outside of their tribe or village was slavery. There were no employer-employee relationships in many societies, which means that anytime a person worked outside of his family or tribe, it was a form of slavery. Ancient tribes were self-sustaining by the members of the tribe. Tribes swapped with each other; but, there was no traditional employer-employee practice. However, any such method would be seen as slavery, just as our 9 – 5 job.

The concept of black was a strategy employed by white racists to create conflict and control. Africa is a vast continent with about 130 billion individuals. On this continent, people are classified by tribe or geographical location (i.e., Kenyan, Somalian, Sudanese, Libyan, etc.). There was no such thing as a black African or white African. They were simply referred to as Africans; to be specific, they are were identified by the specific country within the continent (not the entire continent).

Colonization and the European slave trade changed this look. Thus, rather than classify Africans based on their culture, languages, or geographical locations, more considerable attention was placed on the colour of the skin.

Europeans were armed with the bible and gun; and enhanced the conflict between the already warring tribes. They were frequently selling weapons to both tribes for slaves held as prisoners of war. Their manipulative version of the bible and religious doctrine often saw the trade and institution as righteous.

These practices are regarded as evil, ungodly, and inhuman treatment of black people. For these reasons, the white racist has held the notion that blacks are uncivilized and will always be regarded as inadequate. Various lectures and speeches made by some of the white leaders have exposed their perception of black people, and this has been reflected in their attitude towards Africans. In many cases, white racists were able to take advantage of the ignorance of Africans taken from their land or born in the colonies by making black people perceive that their African heritage and culture was savage and unsophisticated.

They stripped the Africans of their language, culture, religion, and other aspects of life. Since the African nations became dependent on the slavemaster, they had to view themselves and the world through the lens of their captors. Servitude and survival became synonymous.

The European trans-Atlantic slave trade was not just limited to kidnapping and human trafficking; it included the looting of resources, and even actual and constructive enslavement of Africans remaining on the continent

Using skin colour to define ethnic groups is a tactic to impose control and division. Even African Americans of different skin tones are pitted against each other. A method described in the infamous *Willie Lynch Speech* as a method to control black people through division. Divison among African Americans in America is similar to the divisions among Africans on the continent. There is documented proof of a concerted effort to create and capitalize on the division. America can overthrow and control entire countries; however, it cannot control gang violence in America. The proof that African Americans are not seen as Americans; is exemplified by how the gang and other violent issues are seen as black on black and a crisis in black America. If black did not matter, these issues would be addressed as an American crisis, and gang violence would stop tomorrow.

With control, it became easy for the white racist to control the black community. The three metaphorical concepts that are used to control African Americans are the pimp game, the prison yard, and the pocket concept.

The Pimp game: This reflects the relationship between a pimp and the prostitutes he controls. In this type of contact, the pimp creates conflicts between the prostitutes and uses various means to wield his control over them. The prostitutes in their quest to remain the pimp's favourite endure all the inhumane treatment meted out to them. As a means of consoling themselves, some of these prostitutes even boast of being the pimp's favourite.

These victims are aware of all the wrongs they are exposed to and also recognize the importance of the role they play in the pimping business, but the fear of survival and abandonment keeps them with the pimp. These pimps, who are exploiting women, presents one of the prostitutes as his favorite whore and refers to her as the"bottom bitch". While this looks like an elevating position for the bottom bitch, it is just another manipulative strategy the pimp makes use of to take advantage of the prostitute and keeps her depending on him for most of her needs. In doing this, the pimp successfully creates an image in the mind of the prostitute that she needs him for her survival, making it very difficult for her to reach out for her independence. The pimp paints a picture for his victim, making her believe that she must depend on him for all of her needs and security.

Immediately the pimp gets the prostitute to trust him. He takes advantage of her weakness and exploits her to his utmost desire. It is only natural that depending so much on the pimp affects the prostitute's self-esteem. Thus, in no time, she starts feeling inadequate and turns towards the pimp for a reminder of her worth. The pimp, rather than help her develop her self-esteem, would take advantage of her low self-esteem and exploit her. The pimp ensures that the other prostitutes are at loggerheads with one another. While he is solely responsible for all of the disagreements and conflicts they experience, he pretends to be unaware of their plight. He pretends to be a unifying factor in the situation. In this way, he gets the prostitutes to trust him completely. It is at this point that the pimp manipulates their hate and distrust for one another to his advantage. He remains in the background observing the bad blood that exists among them, feigns ignorance, and puts up a white flag in pretence. Unfortunately, the pimps realize that the prostitutes are vulnerable to them and use this to his advantage by manipulating them and making use of every good thing they possess for his selfish gains.

The pimp game is a clear demonstration of the game the so called white elite play on African Americans, white racists, and others. To this effect, they have put a hierarchy in place to support this belief. In this mindset which is really fueled by fear, white racist consider themself to be above other races. Thus, other groups are led to believe that they are not as bad as black people, which is a typical explanation for classifying one of the prostitutes as the "bottom bitch" and creates the division to maintain conflict and control. White racist have successfully instilled negative thoughts and descriptions of the blacks that they have lost identity of who they are. Some black people, irrespective of the terrible treatment they have endured from white racist, still turn to white racist for protection and comfort.

It is evident that white racist have degraded African Americans and made some feel inferior about their race. Rather than stand for themselves and defend themselves, some black Americans turn to white racists for approval. This pimp game is a perfect way to demonstrate the current situation of whites and some black Americans today. White racists have successfully manipulated some black Americans who are dependent on them.

The Prison Yard: In the prison yard, there are hundreds of prisoners that are separated by race; by a small number of officers. Irrespective of their racial differences, it is easy for these prisoners to maintain with one another. Thus, the prison officers resort to the use of conflict to create disagreement between the different races in prisons. As a result of these conflicts introduced by the prison officers, these prisoners refuse to associate with one another. They would instead settle for living in disunity, depending on the nature of the conflict or disagreement. The officers are now able to control the masses and capitalize on the conflict and pseudo-differences between the perceived colors and races. The officer represents people like the Donald Trumps of the world and the prisoners represent poor and working class white racists, black people, and other races.

It has been a clear explanation for the relationship between white racist and other races. Now, the prison yard concept provides a detailed analysis of the system employed by white racist in treating other nationalities. The prison or correction officers represent the so called white elite while the prisoners of different races represent various races in the U.S.. White racist elite are well-aware that irrespective of differences created by nationalities, these prisoners can come together and unite to form a formidable force. They know that such unity can become unsettling and may likely affect their scheme. So, to ensure that this unity never comes to be, they introduce conflict methods among the various nationalities. It is in this tension African Americans, white working class, poor whites, and others continue to be controlled and manipulated.

Pocket concept: President Lyndon B. Johnson once said that " as long as you can convince the lowest white man that he is better than the highest black man, you can keep your hand in his pocket all day long".

Poor and working class white Americans, like the overseer during slavery, must be convinced that black people are beneath them. The establishment and ruling class must control lower class white people; otherwise, white lower class will rebel.

Humans are enticed by power. Inferior people, which includes some lawmakers, police, judges, and prosecutors seek authority to possess power. Power is often confused with respect. Those who crave for power, operate under the attitude that if they cannot get your respect by position of perceived theory, they asset fear.

CHAPTER TWO

WHEN THE JURY COMES BLACK

Primer: Juries determine liability, guilt, or innocence in criminal and civil trials. The jury is composed of citizens, generally untrained in the law, and, after hearing and seeing the evidence, collectively determine the outcome. These citizens, specifically in criminal cases, are to presume the person charged with a crime, not guilty. The presumption of innonce requires two other presumptions: the first is that the police arrested an innocent person; and that the prosecutor and court are attempting to send the wrong person to jail. The general belief that the police do not arrest innocent people or that the courts and prosecutors would not have the wrong person charged is diametrically opposed to the premise that the accused is presumed not guilty. Therefore, the fairest of jurors would have both suspicions of the police and prosecutors. This is heavily based on the perception of people summoned to serve on a jury is based on their experiences.

It is not unusual for African Americans to have a distrust of the police, prosecutors, and the court system. However, many white Americans would not have the same suspicion as black Americans. Black Americans would more likely be best fit as a juror because their distrust would make them prone to presuming innocence. Unfortunately, black Americans experience with law enforcement make them more likely to be excused from juries because many courts see distrust as a base of exclusion under the constitution. After all, they may not correctly analyze the evidence. The real reason why this paradigm becomes the focus of exclusion from the jury is that it makes it harder for the prosecutor to prosecute the accused, whether innocent or guilty.

On the other hand, a white juror with a favourable opinion of police and prosecutors is not seen as being subjected to exclusion under a constitutional challenge. A black defendant would encounter problems in cases where the juries were so reflective. If juries were more representative of the accused's peers, you would see less convictions of innocent people, and more convictions of police officers accused of police misconduct; thus, more justice for black people.

Without jury reform, there will never be a massive and meaningful change in the criminal justice system for African Americans and police brutality.

The Jury system is made up of twelve (12) individuals who make decisions on whether an accused person is guilty or not of an offence. Since the court makes decisions based on two situations, that is, a trial of fact and law, the jury analyzes events as it relates to the law that the judge provides. Thus, the panel is ultimately responsible for the fate of every accused person in the courtroom.

These actions presuppose that the weight of responsibilities attached to the jury can be abused if things are conducted appropriately. The law requires that the panel attends to every case without bias and ensure that justice is served accordingly. The only bias the jury is allowed to have is the presumption of innocence.

Legally, the law states that the Jury system is incorrigible and impartial, considering that the lives of many individuals are linked to the decisions they make. Unfortunately, this is almost impossible to achieve as a majority of the juries are made up of whites. There are many places in the United States where there is hardly a black person chosen to serve as a juror.

Statistically, African Americans are going to have a tough time with a white jury based on their perception of the system and the burden of the prosecutor. Black jurors are more likely to challenge the system, thus making the prosecutor prove all elements of a crime before conviction. Prosecutors know this fact and use it to their advantage in jury selection, and ultimately to convict. This fact also causes many African Americans to take plea deals that they usually would not accept. The ultimate challenge for the black defendant is not whether he is guilty or innocent; it is dealing with the reality that the justice system has nothing to do with guilt or innocence. The issue is whether the court is going to summon a jury of 12 fair jurors who are suspicious of the system; which has proved more than not, unlikely.

The legal system states that a person is supposed to be presumed innocent until proven guilty - emphasizes the premise of the presumption of innocence. It is what makes the difference between being arrested and prosecuted. Thus, when an individual is arrested, such a person is supposed to be still presumed innocent; and, only after the prosecutor (government) proves their case beyond a reasonable doubt at trial can, the charged person be found guilty. However, the reality is that the system is dependent on citizens who know little about the justice system and are contaminated with their own biases based on their own experiences. White people who sit on juries with black defendants are equipped with their eperience and reality. The fact is that a black person's experiences and realities are often different, which often dictates the perception of action or inaction of a defendant. In other words, what may seem genuine and reasonable to a black person may not look natural and understandable to a white person, which causes most black people to be wrongfully convicted, overcharged, and subject to injustice.

The most critical issue in the process of criminal justice is the Jury system. This jury system, which is usually predominately white, consists of individuals who have different perspectives and experiences towards the system. They are likely not to question the system or scrutinize it in a way that would hold the government to its burden of proving the case beyond a reasonable doubt. Reasonableness is subjective and influenced by individual experiences (group experiences are similar along racial lines). African Americans fear for their lives when they appear before the jury. As a result, it causes many black Americans to take plea deals for things they may not have done because they are fearful of going before the court a white jury. The number of wrongful convictions and plea bargains, including the Central Park Five is mind blowing and chilling.

The jury of your peers; the Baston-Wheeler rule

Law clearly states that a person is entitled to a jury that represents a cross-section of his community and that a black juror cannot be excluded based on their race; however, the law has not proved useful in this regard.

The court summons jurors, supposedly, by the use of public rolls like voter registration system or motor vehicle records. How these random lists of jurors are chosen is not indeed known, but typically consist of juries not reflective of the charged defendant or the community.

Also, jury duty often requires a citizen to sit on the jury for days or weeks at a time. Generally, the pay for jury duty is around $20 per day; at that rate, many people are unable to serve because of the financial implications. Most cannot take off of work for that period due to economic reasons; which, plays a significant role in excluding persons from certain social-economic groups that African Americans usually fall in.

The lack of African Americans on jury pools and panels around this country is at the essence of the unfair criminal justice system crisis plaguing the black community. Black leaders, activists, and every black citizen must demand an explanation of the analysis used to choose jury pools and a change in legislation as to how jury pools are summoned, and an evaluation of pay for persons serving on juries. If the jury makeup is changed to reflect African Americans on all panels for which African Americans are charged; you will see a profound change in the criminal justice system.

Although the efforts of the Black Lives Matter movement should be applauded, more would be accomplished if there was a focus on jury reform. Suppose jury commissioners and court supervisors were confronted and held to task about the lack of black representation on jurys.

Many of the African Americans are misinformed or uninformed about the impact of the jury system. It is, therefore, the responsibility of the leaders to ensure that blacks are adequately educated about the impact of the jury system and their need to serve.

For example, Timothy Foster, a black man, was sentenced to death by a white Jury in 1987. In 2016, the case was reviewed by the U.S. Supreme Court. The court opined that the judgment given by the jury was not a fair one. Chief Justice John Roberts, stated that the verdict given to Timothy Foster was based on race. The Chief Justice also mentioned that the injustice frequently imposed on Blacks is because African Americans are often excluded from participating in the Jury system. He noted that it would be near impossible for a black man to be able to enjoy justice if whites dominate the jury system.

Until African Americans collectively advocate for better representation on the jury system, there will be no justice in the criminal justice system for African Americans. Even if you have a black judge, a black defense lawyer, a black prosecutor, a black defendant, and a white jury, you are going to get the same result, and it is called INJUSTICE.

CRIMINAL INJUSTICE:

Arrests: African Americans are much more likely to be arrested by police than White Americans (source: see references).

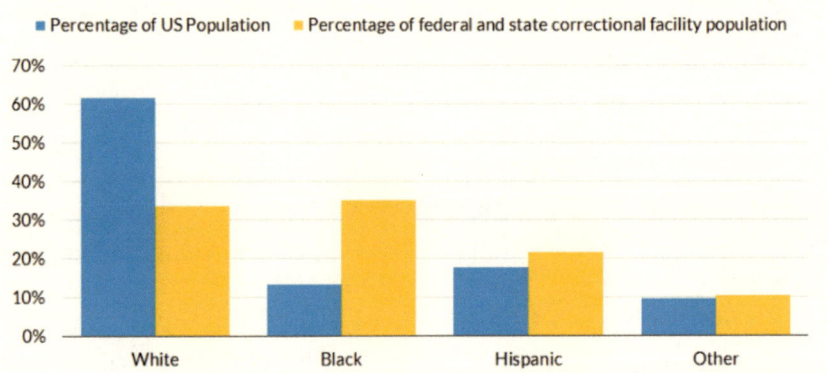

Criminal Justice System Involvement in the United States by Race

Plea Bargains: a graph showing that African Americans are much more likely to take a plea bargain than White Americans(source: see references).

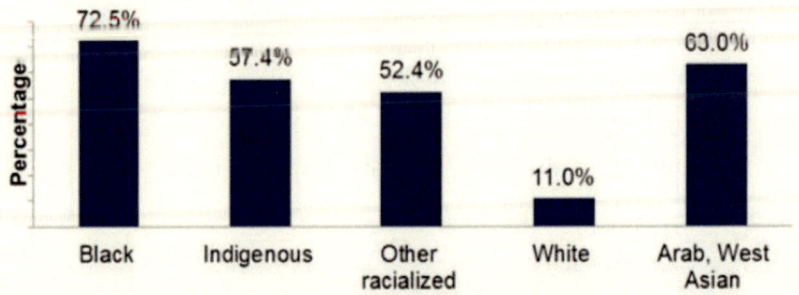

22

Convictions: African Americans are much more likely to be convicted of a criminal offence than White Americans (source: see references).

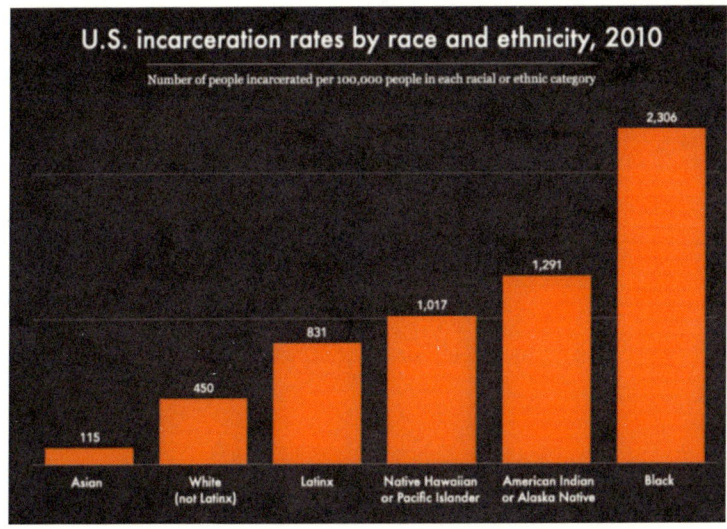

Sentencing: African Americans are much more likely to receive a much l4nger and harsher sentence for the same crime than White Americans (source: see references).

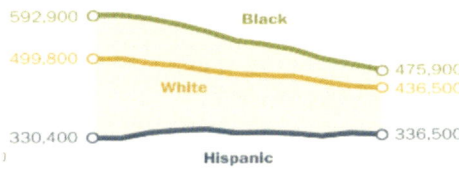

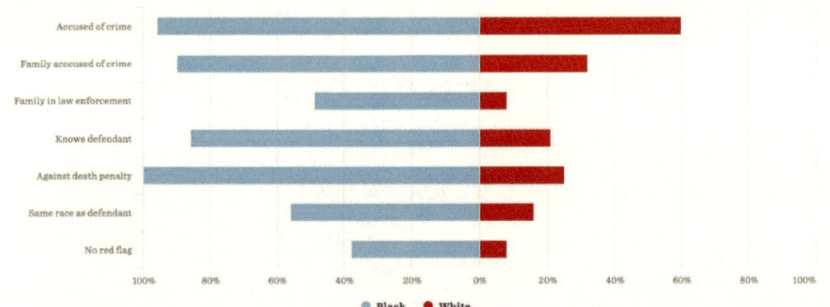

Police Abuse: African Americans are much more likely to be subjected to use of force by police during an arrest than White Americans (source: see references).

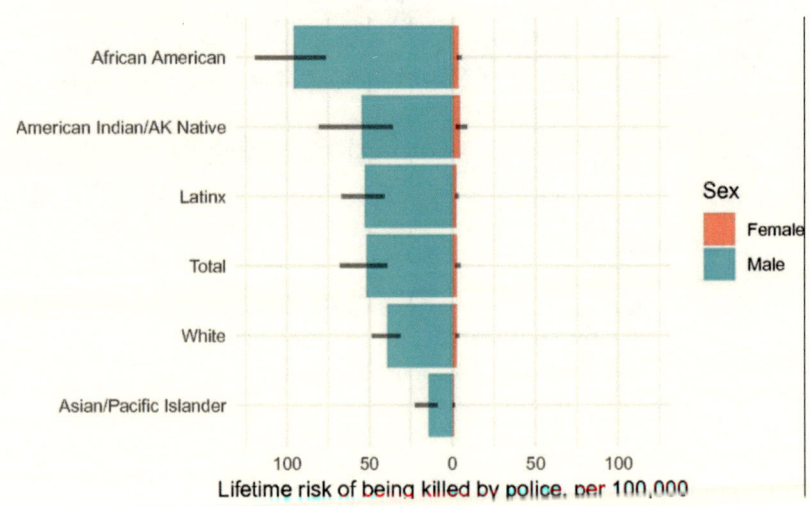

CHAPTER THREE

BUYING BLACK JUSTICE

Primer: The enslavement of African Americans and the geno-cide of Native Americans in North America is well cemented in the annals of world history as the greatest crime against a people in human history. Other situations witnessed were Black codes, black wall street, and the convict lease system. The drugging of black Americans by the CIA and mass killing of Africans were also strategies of economic colonization.

Another case of economic disenfranchisement was when Dr Martin Luther King Jr. was killed in Memphis when he was to partic-ipate in the sanitation workers strike regarding protest of wages; and gearing up for the Poor Peoples March in Washington, D.C.. For years Dr King had advocated for civil rights; however, it was his stance on economic rights that resulted in his assassination.

Economic empowerment for black people would bring true independence and power. As long as black people stand on a weak economic base, they will continue to suffer. Ownership of land and businesses is necessary for black people to gain real power and equal-ity in America. Everything in America is for sell; including, justice and equality.

Prior economy-based solutions for African Americans have primarily focused on consumer power by boycotting and collective focus on buying power. African Americans must concentrate on ownership instead of consumerism. Although America was indeed built on the backs of black Americans, it is a reality that African Americans must have ownership in the house to get a seat at the table. Unless African Americans focus on creating weath and ownership, instead of solely consumer power, black people will not see justice.

There must be a sacrifice made to build more wealth and ownership. Most businesses fail within three years; and, obtaining capital to start a business can also be very challenging. However, collectively, African Americans have the money; the issue is connecting and being resilient in building and buying. The fallacy is the need for one black leader to accomplish this plan. The need for leadership causes more inaction than progress. African Americans must move individually with a collective plan; instead of following as a group with an individual focus. African Americans need to focus on teaching future generations to focus on ownership and independence instead of being an employee.

Economic Colonialism (European Colonization of Africa and the Americas; and the transatlantic slave trade) had the primary purpose of exploiting the natural resources of the continent, the genocide of the indigenous subjects, and exploitation of human capital (specifically the Africans). Throughout American history, the oppression of black people was and is a casualty of economic colonialism. Again, economic empowerment is necessary with a focus on business development and ownership. Money caused the problem, and money will solve the problem with less emphasis on consumerism; and a focus on property ownership and entrepreneurship. This will solve and rectify the crisis in black America.

African Americans lag behind all other groups in the economic framework of America. A large number of African Americans experience financial hardship and struggle to make ends meet. Countless African Americans are unemployed, underemployed, and unemployable; the same is true regardless of education, skill, or experience. With businesses, African Americans can establish an employment base.

Economic colonialism and how it relates to African slavery in North America

Human capital is the most essential and expensive cost of any business. Labour costs generally account for more than fifty percent of the business's overall costs and expense. Cheap labour is a commodity that bleeds richness. But, no charge for work would almost guarantee wealth. When the Europeans sent colonists to North America, it was not to seek freedom; it was to make money for the European power.

Wealthy plantation owners, and some not so wealthy, went to slave auctions to purchase human capital to work for free. These African slaves brought to North America were shackled, chained, and sold on the auction block. Buying a human being to slave for you seems like a win-win; however, there is, was one problem: how do you control a human that does not want to be a slave? You beat him until he accepts it. Just like the pimp game. How does a pimp make a woman like selling her body? He mentally manipulates her; and, if that does not work, he beats it into her. It was not easy being a plantation owner with slaves. Making sure that your human capital would submit and not kill you, you had to master the process of taming them. Some people specialized in taming slaves; others were employed as overseers. Similar techniques are taught and used by the military and intelligence agencies around the world. The creation of submissive human resources would enable the slaves to work without complaints, revolts, or resignation (runaway). The primary objective of the above strategy was to make the slaves accomplish the wants of their bosses.

The slave trade was purely an economic situation. Africans, who were used as slaves, generated money for their colonial masters. Like all pimps, they have to justify using prostitutes to make money. You have to establish order among the slaves, overseers, merchants, family members, friends, and associates. How do you determine the legitimacy of what you are doing? How do you maintain dignity while doing such a vile and disgusting thing like enslaving human beings? How do you make the white overseer of your slaves control humans? You create a narrative that justifies what you are doing. You dehumanize the slave. Just like a pimp would not prostitute his mother or sister. How does he justify prostituting someone else's mother or sister? He relegates her to less than human, labels her a"whore". She is not a lady; she is just a"whore". If you propagate a social narrative that relegates the African slave as a less than human, you can justify it with the other slaves, overseer, merchants, family, friends, associates, and the community in which you live. But, most importantly, you justify it with the slave that you own. A person who believes that he should be free and is equal will never mentally submit to bondage. Just like the pimp makes the prostitute believe she needs him; there is a process to take away the self-esteem.

Socially, owning slaves was seen as prestigious and sign of wealth. Many slaves, over centuries, made many colonists wealthy. Going into the twentieth century, except for stealing the land from native Americans, free – uncompensated slave labour accounted for the most critical institution that made America the most powerful nation in the world. That is still true today.

Humans can only be owned if they are property. The more slaves a white slave owner possess, the higher his social status.

The government also thrived on accounts of slave trades, and in no time, taxes were levied on the various transactions that involved slaves. Now the government was in on it. Like any exchange of goods and services, charges could be levied against the purchase and selling of slaves. Slaves could also be used to satisfy tax liens, making the slave property of the government, who could sell the slave to satisfy the claim. Slaves could increase and decrease in value. A young slave could be bought cheaply and sold at adulthood after they were tamed and experienced. Females slaves, who were raped as children, could be used to entertain guests and even generate revenue for sex.

It would not only be the private slave owner who profited; it was also the government, banks; and, even insurance companies that insured the slave as property.

The American Revolution was a fight over money. The colonists were tired of being taxed by the British and wanted to keep more of their revenue.

Slave Laws Enacted to Protected The Human Capital of the Colonists

Slave laws were enacted to regulate slavery. The essence of these laws was to place restrictions on the rights of Africans; to protect the economic interest of the colonists. It also mandated that slaves were only to obey the commands of their masters without asking questions.

Consequently, the slaves who gained freedom from their masters did not enjoy "free" lives. They found it difficult to secure any suitable employment as a result of their previous status as slaves. The economic situation made it so difficult for African Americans to enjoy the same privileges as their white counterparts because they had endured so many years of slavery. During their periods as slaves, they had already contributed to the development of America. Even employment for a

29

former slave was generally for small wages and the same type of work and treatment. In essence, when an African American wanted to work and make a living, he still had to go back to the colonial master to work.

Key: The only way for a former slave to achieve a status of independence was to own his plantation.

How the Emancipation of slaves and subsequent 13th amendment, Black Codes, and Convict Lease System contributed to Economic Colonialism in North America (1863 to early 1900s)

President Abraham Lincoln issued the Emancipation Proclamation in 1863, freeing persons held as slaves within the rebellious states. It only applied to slaves held within the rebellious states. It was the most effective way to break the South. First, the South had an economy that depended on slave labour, unlike the North, who had become industrialized, and, Second, slave ownership continued to be a symbol of status.

However, after the Emancipation Proclamation, former slaves primarily worked as sharecroppers or in a subservient capacity. Additionally, vagrancy laws and other ordinances were enacted to specifically criminalize African Americans so that they would be arrested, jailed, and leased out to plantations under similar conditions as slavery.

Two years after the issuance of the Emancipation Proclamation, the 13th amendment of the U.S. Constitution was enacted, which prohibited slavery, except for conviction of a crime.

Under sharecropping, undesirable working conditions, and convict lease system; many African Americans would not be able to truly enjoy freedom, unless they owned their property and business.

How Jim Crowism and focus on Civil rights, Black Power, and Boycotting contributed to Economic Colonialism in North America (early 1900s to 1960s)

In 1896, the U.S. Supreme Court in Plessy vs Ferguson ruled that the separation of blacks was not unconstitutional, as long as the facilities and institutions were equal, known as the separate but equal doctrine; birthing the Jim Crow era.

Jim Crow was a pivotal point because many black leaders believed that full integration with white Americans would solve the separate but equal problem, and political, social, and economic equality would follow. In 1954, the U.S. Supreme Court heard the case of Brown vs Board of Education, with civil rights attorney Thurgood Marshall arguing for the Plaintiffs. The court overruled Plessy and found that the separate but equal doctrine was unconstitutional.

Armed with Plessy, for decades, black leaders and advocates focused on the integration of blacks into white America, including voting, education, and employment. Blacks, who generally had no wealth, focused on boycotting instead of ownership. For example, imagine if in the infamous Rosa Parks bus strike, if African Americans concentrated on buying and operating its bus system instead of advocating for sitting at the front of a white-owned bus.

Except for the Nation of Islam, who focused on building wealth with success; no black group focused extensively on building wealth with success. Marcus Garvey does get an honorable mention. Civil rights groups focused on integration; black power and nationalists groups focused on nationalism, socialism, and back to Africa agendas without money; and others enjoyed just being left alone while they worked for white folks. None of these strategies proved to have a profound impact.

Accomodationalists and integrationists are still arguing for the same political integration; black power and nationalists groups, although conscious, are non-existent and vastly ineffective as to real change; and those just fine with working master's house are not woke. Many of the ownership conscious black Americans, understand money, but not economics. Within the black community, individuals have achieved massive success in business and entertainment; however, group economics still eludes African Americans.

Economic independence does not necessarily mean that a person has more net worth or assets than anyone else; it implies that the person is positioned to not rely on others for survival; specifically, groups who have oppressed them. As a group, the focus is not to only build wealth; it is to develop independence. White racist prefer selling of businesses that would, in turn, promote the taking of good welfare of the whites as a sign of power, which is bias. They do not see any loss even if it does yield monetary benefit in the short term.

Many prominent black-owned businesses have failed or sold to white-owned companies. While specific individuals may have realized a financial benefit, the group suffers. Frequently, this is the result of the failure of black consumers to support black businesses. The belief that white companies are offering more convenient or better services and goods is often inaccurate and a misconception perpetuated by the slave mentality. African Americans tend to perceive that services are better and tolerate more from white businesses. African Americans believe that a white service or business will be more reliable and beneficial. Even when black people are used for service and goods, they are often backed by white-owned companies as an agent or subsidiary.

Group economics include starting a business, employing black workers, supporting black-owned businesses, supporting black schools, using black banks, and starting black investment groups.

African Americans should provide workshops and focus on improving the understanding of economics for the youth and others in the community.

African Americans have $1.3 trillion in buying power. The buying dollars in black America rarely circulate within the community. With that buying power, black people could command and gain equality in the land of economics. In America, no money equals no power.

Group economics is when one group of people have a common economic interest and actively and consciously agree to pursue an independent industrial base. Without group economics, black Americans will not see independence, power, and equality.

J. Edgar Hoover's COINTELPRO and Economic Colonialism (1950s to 1970s)

J. Edgar Hoover, former Director of the Federal Bureau of Investigations, played a critical and vital role in maintaining the social order established in early colonial America. COINTELPRO (Counter Intelligence Program) was established by J. Edgar Hoover, after Brown v. Board of Education and continued until the end of the Civil Rights movement. The timing was not accidental, as it was created after the Supreme Court decision in Brown. The primary purpose and impact were to destroy anyone, particularly in the black community, that interfered with social order established before Brown. In essence, it sought to prevent any advancement of African Americans, who had been effectively second class citizens and a permanent underclass. Cloaked as a project to stop threats against the United States, it was genuine from the perspective that black equality was and is a threat to white racist Americans.

Reaganomics, Drugging Black America, War on Drugs, Mass Incarceration, and Making America Great Again (1980s to 2020)

During Reagan's presidency, black America, saw many African Americans find success in politics, entertainment, and business. However, black unemployment reached its highest level since the emancipation proclamation. In essence, Reagan solidified the ineffectiveness of black tokenism. The position does not mean power. Regardless of how many blacks are elected to office or elevated to prominent positions, if the black community fails to establish robust group economics, there will be no true equality.

To circumvent the alarming unemployment rate, black America witnessed an expansion in drug addiction, which created a market for drug sales. The 1980s is known as the start of the"crack era" which is used to describe the period in which the country saw an explosion in the black community experiencing a massive drug addiction crisis, so-called black on black crime and violence, family breakdown, and decay of the community conditions. The country watched as a segment of its citizens was self-destructing, with much help from the government.

The government proved to be one of the biggest culprits in the decay of black inter-city in the 1980s. The Central Intelligence Agency needed financial support to bankroll the contras in South America. To get money, the CIA and DEA funnelled drugs into the community as its source of generating the revenue needed. While the CIA and DEA were funnelling drugs into black America, President Reagan and his wife, Nancy Reagan, were launching their Just Say No campaign. In 1986, Congress passed the Anti-Drug Abuse Act, which called for massive mandatory prison sentences, which differentiated between drugs. For example, crack cocaine, used more often by black Americans, resulting in longer and harsher prison sentences than powder cocaine, which was more commonly used by white Americans. As a result, the prison population increased almost tenfold from the time Reagan started the so-called war on drugs (which was a war on black America) to a decade later (the mid-1990s).

The war on illegal drugs promoted the need to search for more slaves. Nevertheless, President Bill Clinton's Violent Crime Control and Law enforcement Act expanded the prison industrial complex. The prison has become the new plantation, and black Americans, have become the new slaves.

The prison industrial complex and mass incarceration resemble slavery and the convict lease system. Although President Trump has signed the bill abolishing the Clinton era crime bill, he had reminded America just how great it was when it enslaved, leased, Jim Crowed, drugged, imprisoned, and COINTELPROed black America. Trump, through his actions, encited and encouraged the police to continue with their practice of slave patrols by killing black men and women, on and off camera, without cause or justification.

The clear lesson is that black America must build a solid economic base to deal with the massive crisis of social and economic inequality in black America. African Americans cannot ignore our leaders who promote economic empowerment like Dr Claud Anderson, who wrote Powernomics, a must-read for all black people. The right to go to integrated schools, restaurants, and work will not translate to equality and justice for black people. Marching, boycotting, and lobbying will only get black people to the front door and an invite in the house to sit at the table. Group economics will get black people the deed to the house.

ECONOMICS:

Unemployment: African Americans unemployment rate is much higher than White Americans (source: see references).

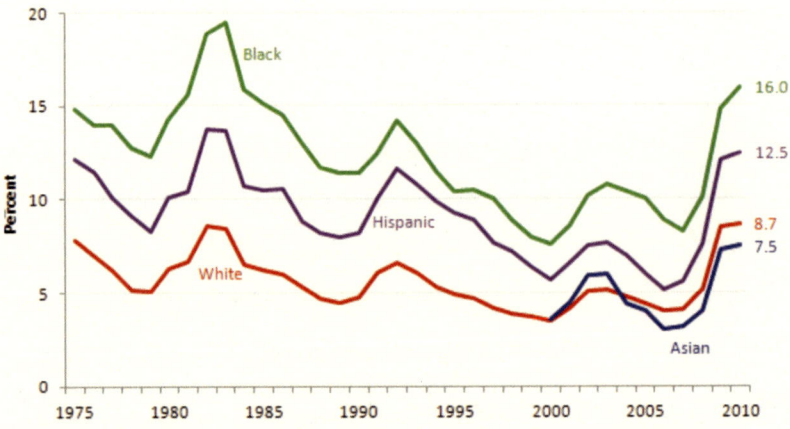

Income: African Americans average salary is much lower than White Americans (source: see references).

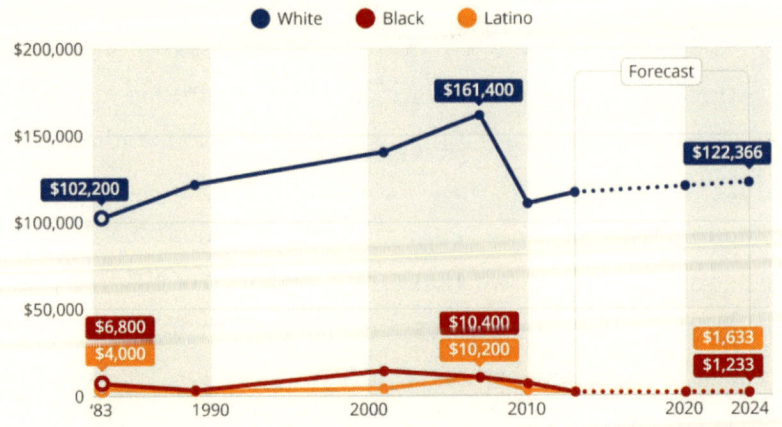

Business Ownership: African American business ownership rate is much lower than White Americans (source: see references).

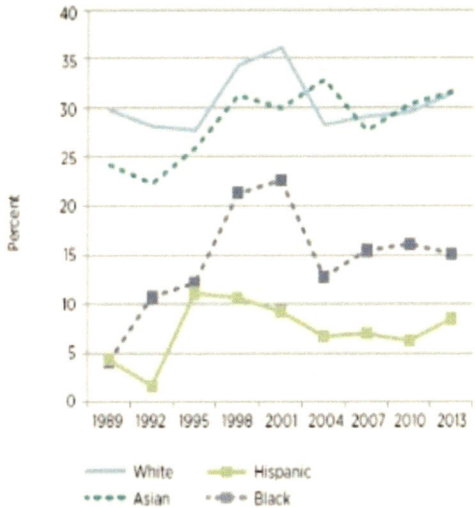

Loans: African Americans are less likely than white Americans to be approved for a loan (source: see references).

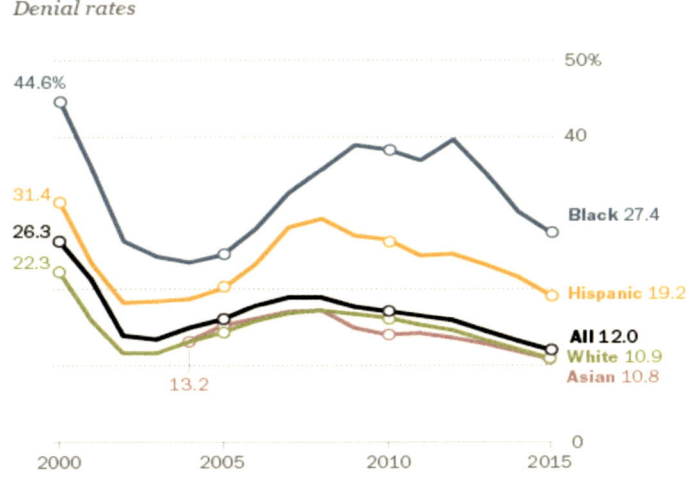

Denial rates

Note: Data based on applications for conventional loans for one-to-four-family home purchases, including manufactured homes. Data on Asians were not broken out separately until 2004. Hispanics may be of any race.

Home Ownership: African Americans are less likely than white Americans to own a home (source: see references).

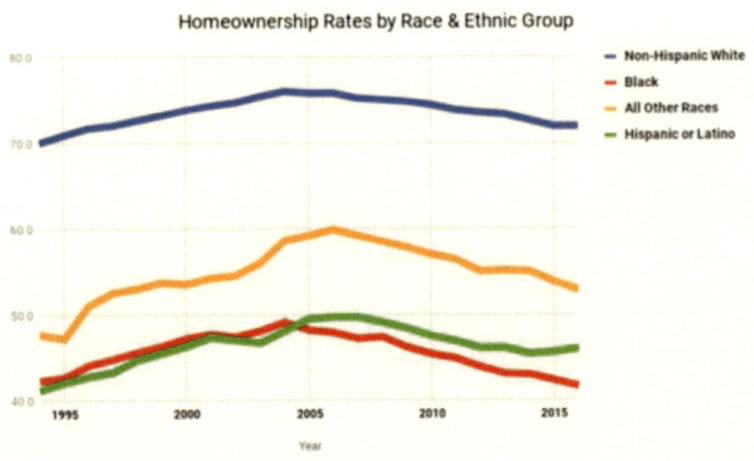

Net Worth (source: see references).

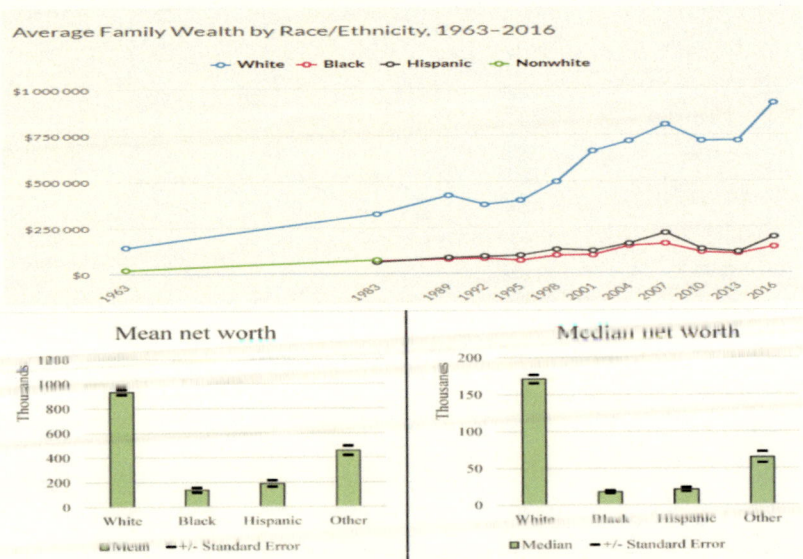

CHAPTER FOUR

THE PAY BLACK

When enslaved Africans were freed after the emancipation proclamation, slave owners were given reparations for each slave in an amount that equals approximately $10,000.00 per slave today. There were approximately 3,953,762 slaves in America at the time of the civil war. Do the math. However, America compensated the slave owner, but nothing for the slave. YET?

Under any standard of human rights law, the practice of slavery in the United States was a gross human rights violation and criminal; and some form of sanctions and restitution is owed to the slaves and their descendants. The United States practices of racial separation and discrimination against the descendants of former slaves during the century after the emancipation proclamation alone is a gross human rights violation and criminal; and some form of sanctions and restitution is owed to the descendants of slaves.

The United States has paid reparations to many groups that have suffered less, including the Japanese. So why not reparations to the descendants of former slaves? The payment of any meaningful reparations to African Americans would shift everything in America. Capitalism, as a monetary system, generates massive wealth; however, it requires poverty. Either resource is distributed equally, which theoretically makes everyone equal (socialism); or, resources are distributed unequally (capitalism). If funds are shifted favourably towards African Americans, who loses? If black people are given a significant economic boost and capitalize on the increase, there would be an economic power in a group of people that were chained and shackled for four centuries. The entire American system would shift. A substantial financial shift in favour of black people would mean a disfavorable economic change for white people.

Non-European immigrants do not want what African Americans deserve. Also, non-European immigrants are controlled and complacent to social order. Non-European immigrants that achieve economic success are of no threat to the descendants, accomplices, and conspirers of the North American slave crime. There is an inherent fear of any human that has wronged a person. Pharoah's acts of oppression were fueled by fear of people he abused and their descendants. In 1921 in the Greenwood District in Tulsa, Oklahoma, where there was a thriving black community, white racists and the National Guard embarked on an unprovoked terrorist attack against the black community, destroying land, businesses, and killing innocent back people. Why? Fear of rising.

During the years of the emancipation proclamation, Congress and the Freedman's Bureau discussed what they would do with the former slaves. Specifically, they debated about the social and economic status of the former slaves. It is well documented that land and money were acknowledged as critical to the former slave's freedom. The War Department had an approved plan to distribute land and property to the former slaves; however, President Lincoln was shot, and President Jackson killed the bill.

Reparations for black folks are long overdue. Opponents to reparations, black and white, are strangely misguided, uninformed, unempathetic, and shallow. How black people decide to spend the money is not a reason to deny it. However, much can be said to make sure that African Americans do not waste or give the money back. Building a stable economic base is more critical than reparations.

Frankly, the money owed to black people for its labour and mistreatment would break the bank. There has been much talk about filing charges and seeking restitution with international tribunals like the United Nations and International Criminal Court. Without question, the laws of these tribunals have sanctioned and ordered return for less; however, America would disagree to be held to the power of these tribunals; and, certainly would not comply. Power speaks to power; and, none of these tribunals is powerful enough to do anything with the United States. It would be just a figurehead at best.

Shortly before the assassination of Malcolm X (El Hajj Malik El Shabazz), he advocated for filing charges with the United Nations against the United States government. No one doubt Malcolm's seriousness and intent to get justice for a people who have suffered for so long. However, the sad reality is that the United Nations is a puppet of the United States. Any criticism by a U.N. official is nothing more than rhetoric that may be worth a story heading or sound bite.

African Americans are deserving of reparations, and such advocacy should continue. However, black people must recognize that nobody is going to save you. Understand that group economics is vital, necessary, and a must for black justice.

H.R. 40, also known as The African American Act, was enacted to identify slaves and descendants of slaves; and to establish reparation proposals. We need action; not a study. As Dr. Martin Luther King, Jr. once stated, after explaining land grands and subsidies given to other people who did far less to nothing in comparison to African Americans, "we are coming for our check"

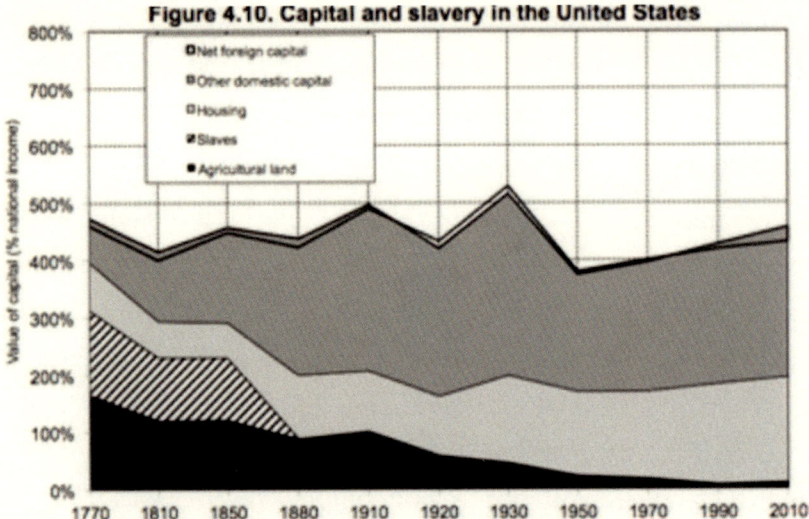

Figure 4.10. Capital and slavery in the United States

The market value of slaves was about 1.5 years of U.S. national income around 1770 (as mush as land).
Sources and series: see piketty.pse.ens.fr/capital21c.

(graph source: see references)

CHAPTER FIVE

WHEN THE VOTES, VALUES, AND PRIDE COME BLACK

The Fifteenth Amendment to the U.S. Constitution supposedly prohibits the federal government from denying a citizen the right to vote based on race, colour, or prior servitude.

Five years after the Civil War, Hiram Rhodes Revels, from Mississippi, became the first black person in Congress. In many parts of the country, the population of blacks often outnumbered whites, particularly in the South. It was seen as a threat to white racist control; and, a new fear of a power shift. White racist Southerners began to start organizations like the White League and others to persecute black people to prevent them from voting. Also, black codes, which were laws made to criminalize acts of blacks only and Jim Crow, allowed white racists to implement measures to make it almost impossible for blacks to vote. For example, would-be black voters were required to pay money (called a poll tax) to vote. Understanding that the former slaves and their descendants were generally poor and could not afford it, black people were prevented from voting. Other measures, such as literacy tests, were also implemented to suppress and prevent African Americans from voting or even registering. From 1901 to 1973, there were no black people elected to Congress from the former confederate states.

During the aftermath of the Brown vs Board of Education, much effort was put into fighting systems that prevented black people from registering and casting votes. There was much bloodshed and lives lost during this struggle.

Ultimately, the Voting Rights Act was passed in 1965. The struggle for the act is heavily attributed to Dr Martin Luther King, Jr.; and signed by President Lyndon B. Johnson. This forced the states that were systematically preventing would-be black voters from registering and voting to change their practices.

Today, gerrymandering and less apparent methods are used to prevent the registration and voting of black Americans. There has been progress, but, unfortunately, the two-party system has not been very beneficial to black people. After integration, many black Americans have become more fragmented and vote individually and not as a group. While it is true that most African Americans vote along party lines, the power of the vote is limited because the voting habits of black America is taken for granted, and little is done politically.

The black vote helped many black political figures get elected in local, state, and federal elections. In 2008, America saw its first black president and first lady in the election of Barack Obama. Due much to the political process, the overall conditions of black Americans saw little change. Black Americans vote with no collective strategy. Also, black people have no lobby with economic clout. Yes, in America, politicians even cost money. Politicians cater to lobby groups who advocate for a cause and contribute to campaigns. In theory, it would be illegal for a group to pay a politician for a favour. However, in practice, campaign contributions are generally not given without some expectation of return. Local, state, and federal politicians receive campaign donations from citizens and groups based on the idea of supporting campaign costs. If you have no money, you cannot run. Common sense, wealthy business people or their lobby are not going to give money to a politician just because he is doing his civic duty. The Boys and Girls Club of America would be a much better choice for donating money to a good cause.

If all a politician needs is your vote and all he or she has to do is tell you what you want to hear without giving you almost nothing in return, you are irrelevant. However, when your vote and lobby are grouped without demands, your interest has been purchased. Free tickets for admission gets you a"nose-bleed sea"; VIP gets you to access to the main act.

There has been much debate over which party has the black interest and should we not vote along party lines. Regardless of the effort, the reality is that black people have to do it as a group; however, it must be in such a way that black people demand results. For example, there is much talk about the presidency of Barack Obama. His administration is historical and momentous, and, for all practical purposes, he held the house together and faced fierce opposition to his plans and agenda. He was a class act that did not embarrass black people. The critics argue that he did little for black America. In other words, we must focus on a black agenda instead of black tokenism. Black America is too obsessed with black firsts; and, continue to be hoodwinked by not getting little to nothing from our black politicians.

Do African Americans demand politicians to articulate a pro gressive black agenda before we give them our vote? Can they just get us with a black running mate and promises unlikely to materialize?

Black people must simultaneously commit themselves to group economics and voting. Cast their dollars and votes in the right place, and mind the shop. Voting and Economics is a collective power.

Donald Trump succeeded Barack Obama as president of the United States. His campaign, election, and tenure as president has symbolized the fear of racist white Americans of a paradigm shift. His success has been largely attributed to black Americans failure to vote. Lack of group voting and involvement in the process will surely have a negative impact on black Americans. Group voting is essential.

VOTING:

African American voting (graph source: see references).

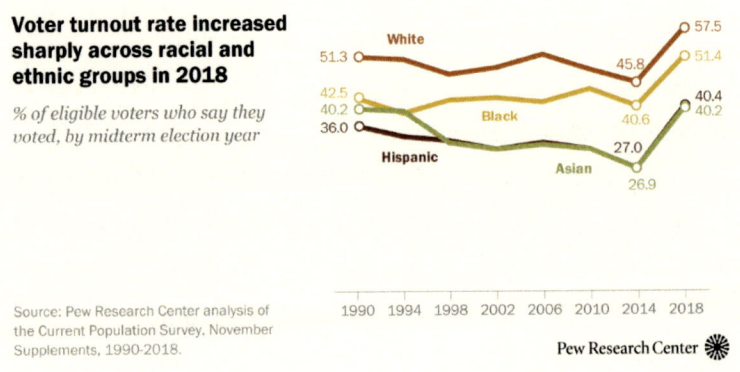

Voter turnout rate increased sharply across racial and ethnic groups in 2018

% of eligible voters who say they voted, by midterm election year

White

51.3

42.5
40.2
36.0

Hispanic

Black

45.8

40.6

27.0

Asian

26.9

57.5

51.4

40.4
40.2

Source: Pew Research Center analysis of the Current Population Survey, November Supplements, 1990-2018.

1990 1994 1998 2002 2006 2010 2014 2018

Pew Research Center

VALUES AND PRIDE

The portrayal of black Americans in film, music, T.V., and popular culture as savages and lacking morals has been a collective and concerted effort to create a narrative and justify the systematic mistreatment of black Americans. To counter this effort, activists, parents, leaders, and black Americans, in general, must focus on rebuilding a healthy value system.

The Birth Of A Nation, which was first called The Clansman, is a 1915 movie made by D.W. Griffith. The movie negatively portrayed

African Americans as savages. It was screened at the White House and is attributed to rebirthing the Ku Klux Klan and adding fuel to fear of blacks. It established the power of media on ideas, attitudes, and social order to promote the business on black Americans.

African Americans have been portrayed in America as irresponsible and a bad influence on society. The various forums the media has used to describe African Americans negatively. The black community is usually represented as a community filled with morally bankrupt individuals. The different music and movies that are used to depict the African American culture say nothing good about African Americans. The white racists have painted an unpleasant picture of the black community. In this way, they hope to justify the ill-treatment of black Americans. All African Americans much watch the Spike Lee classic Bamboozled.

The debate within the community is focused on the irresponsibility of black artists and how they choose to portray black people. Again, due to the lack of black own media forums, black Americans generally have to get the approval of a white-owned media forum to get the budget and access to make music and film. Again, ownership is key.

Black parents, teachers, and leaders must focus on countering the current culture, which depicts blacks in a negative light. Destruction of the black family had been the practice and norm against black people since the enslavement of Africans by Europeans on the American continent.

Many black families were separated and sold off to different plantations. The black family was even more divided as a result of the ever-increasing black incarceration rate.

In 1965 Daniel Moynihan studied the family structure, which he published in The Moynihan report. In 1965, the number of out of wedlock births was twenty-five percent (25%). In the 1990s, after the crack era and crime bill to incarcerate more black people, the out of wedlock births in black America has increased to seventy percent (70%).

Black babies need the love, support, and teachings of two parents. Before segregation took hold, babies born out of wedlock were relatively low. Today, after blacks fled the South to integrate up North and get better jobs, the values of the home did not always go with it.

Africans who were kidnapped and brought to the Americas were not just Africans. They were Africans who survived the middle passage, slavery and bondage for centuries, and the aftermath. African Americans do not only descend from Africans; they descend from Africans who survived the greatest crime against people in human history. Black people should embrace that honour and restore their pride, dignity, and respect. It begins with the black family – black parenthood. Teach the babies.

Historically, African culture is notable for strong family ties, and this is evident in the various activities that members of the families enjoy. Before the slave trade era, the different families in Africa have an organized way of going about their duties and responsibilities. The mother's role was to take good care of the children and the home. She was also expected to provide support to the husband and see that the children were well-taken care.It was also the job of the mother to ensure that the children are taught the right values that are instrumental for societal development and growth.

On the other hand, the children ensured that they obeyed their parents and assisted with the necessary house chores. They are also taught at a very tender age how to comport themselves in public and assume various gender roles. These children are also aware that their parents had the right to punish them whenever they did something inappropriate.

The father in African homes is regarded to be the head of the house. He often earned the title by going through rights of passage; that test to prove he is worthy of transitioning from a boy to a Man. He was not a dictator, and he was a supporter, leader, and provider. He was an example for his boys and a protector for his girls. The father and mother are the first examples of how you should live.

If you want to destroy the family, take the father out of the house. It is wrong not to say that a single mother cannot raise a family because countless black women have done it; and done it well. Women are the most vital part of this process; however, single-parent homes should be an anomaly, not a norm. When you have men in most homes, they serve as an example for the entire community, not just their own home.

A study from the U.S. Department of Health and Human Services concluded that fatherless children are at a dramatically higher risk of drug and alcohol abuse. (National Center for Health Statistics. Survey on Child Health. U.S. Department of Health and Human Services. 1993.) the absence of fathers from the lives of their children has done more harm than good. It can be argued that many of the crisis impacting the African American family is the absence of the father.

It has become too common to see African American homes with only one parent. One parent households are more vulnerable to poverty, unemployment, substance abuse, unplanned pregnancy, and other vices; including:

- Suicide: 63 percent of youth suicides
- Runaways: 90 percent of all homeless and runaway youths
- Behavioral Disorders: 85 percent of all children that exhibit behavioural disorders
- High School Dropouts: 71 percent of all high school dropouts

- Juvenile Detention Rates: 70 percent of juveniles in state-operated institutions

- Substance Abuse: 75 percent of adolescent patients in substance abuse centres

- Aggression: 75 percent of rapists motivated by displaced anger

Black America must focus on the family and maintaining self-pride and dignity. African Americans come from greatness and have a rich culture that has influenced and inspired people around the globe. Embrace it, love it, and carry it with pride.

A significant discussion is black on black crime. While it is true that black people commit most homicides against black people, it is equally valid that white people commit most homicides against white people. Black on black homicides has decreased by approximately seventy percent (70%) in the last twenty years.

Lastly, addiction, poverty, and scarcity of resources, even among wealthy blacks, continues to be a catalyst towards hatred and jealousy within the black community. Black success can be stifled by other black people who are jealous of their success. Haters are a normal part of success; however, marginalized groups, like African Americans, must see the bigger picture. Since slavery, white racists have capitalized on these conflicts and have used them to maintain control of black people. Read the Willie Lynch Speech. Stop hating on each other. One person's success is not your failure.

Discipline, focus, and drive is necessary. The author may lose some readers; however, it must be emphasized that drug and excessive alcohol use must be avoided at all cost. African Americans cannot afford the ultimate cost self medication. Black people must stay clear and focused. Both men and women must focus on the children and youth in the community. It takes both parents and a village to raise a child. Honor, respect, and value parents and our elders; but, we must make sure that we give our youth something to respect.

FAMILY:

Fatherless African American households (graph source: see references).

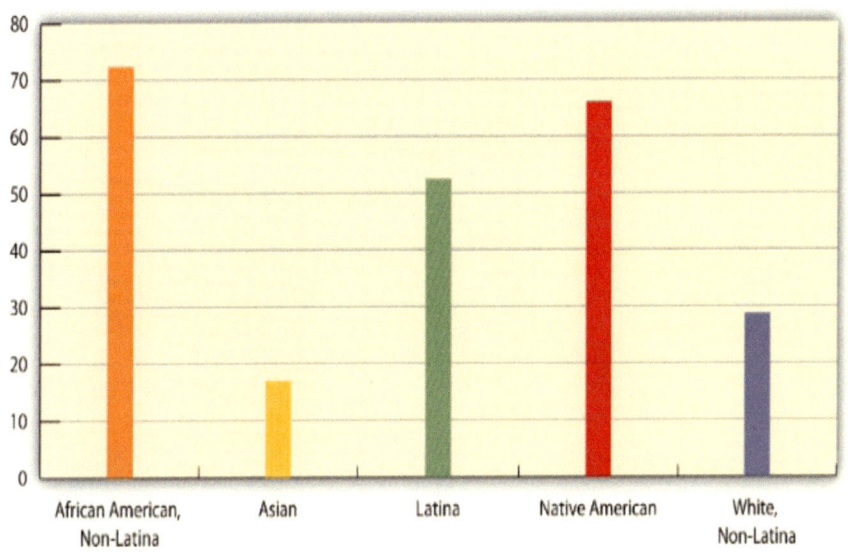

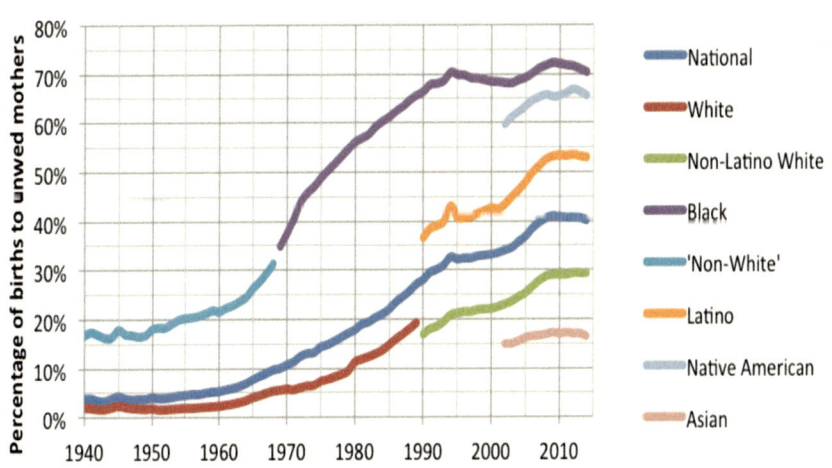

Fatherless inmates (graph source: see references).

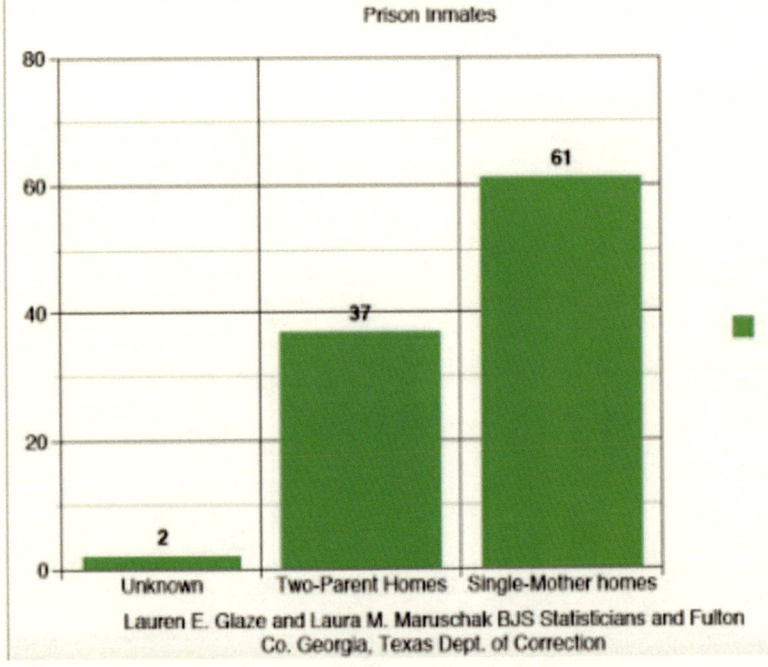

Prison inmates

Lauren E. Glaze and Laura M. Maruschak BJS Statisticians and Fulton
Co. Georgia, Texas Dept. of Correction

CHAPTER SIX

BLACK POWER MATTERS

If black America is ever to gain the justice and power it seeks and deserves, it must focus on economic independence by engaging in massive group economics, consistent group voting, and lobby; and focusing on family, by parenting and valuing self through pride.

Again, nobody is going to save black America. Don't look left or right. Do not look for the next Malcolm or Martin. Do not wait for white Americans to do something. Do your part. Move and don't give up when it gets tough or it seems like the world is against you. Black people are the most spiritual God fearing people on the planet; but, often tend to lose faith quickly. The time is now to do YOUR part. Stop asking other people what they have done for the community. Nobody needs a qualifier. Throwing shade and questioning other people's black card is cooning at its finest. If you troll other black people and complain about what they have not done for their people, you are a bonafide coon. Do your part. Talk about what you do; not what someone else is doing. Hating, questioning, and trolling others is what the slave master taught us to do. These people hate other black people's success.

Black people have created this space where they believe that only so many black people can occupy at the same time. Many black people see other black people's success as their failure. This is a slave self esteem psychosis. Understand your circumstances, do your part, and success will follow. Start your own, do your own, and help like minded people in the community. Black people have been taught to hate each other since their arrival on the continent. The biggest challenge is to stop hating on one another; and focus on what is needed to progress and move forward. Black Nationalist vs. so called Uncle Toms; Conservatives vs. Liberals; Men vs. Women; your neighborhood (you don't own) vs. their neighborhood (they don't own); blood vs. crip; frat vs frat; soror vs soror; light vs. dark; young vs. old; interracial vs. pure black; and it goes on and on. Stop it. Stop doing the white racists job and self destruction over divisions that are irrelevant and superficial. Focus on building and not self destructing.

Black men and women who or vocal and truly speak out for equality and progress have become targets for white racists. However, many black Americans do not effectively support many of the men and women who are on the front lines trying to make a difference. Sometimes African Americans tend to support black people who get the nod from white America. Often, it is white Americans who choose black leaders. Some black people are impressed by black Americnas who are selected and placed in so called prestigious positions; seeing it as a sign of success. Black people often do not give the same nod to those who are primiarily accepted in black circles; especially those that may attract negative attention from white people.

For example, Judge Olu Stevens from Kentucky admonished a white prosecutor for systematically striking black jurors; as a result, the Judge was reprimanded for this act. Very few black Americans spoke on the issue or went to protest for him. He put it on the line for justice; and received little backing. We must support those who support us; especially those in sensitive postions.

Social media has become a platform for some black people to disrespect and dismiss other black people. If a black person is trying to do something positive; acknowledge it and add to it. If you don't like what they are doing, you do something better. Do not criticize black people for trying. Just because you can't do it, don't mean it can't be done. If black people spent as much time talking about what they are doing, opposed to what other people are doing, black America would move forward in leaps and bounds. Black America has a crisis that only black America will be able to fix.

If black people are going to stop our black men and women from getting killed in the streets by white and black racist police officers; and being overcharged, falsely accused, and sentencing to excessive time in jail; black people must get involved in the process. Demand a seat on the jury box. If you are going to allow white people to come into Compton, Inglewood, and so many other places in America and make decisions about black people's fate, then how do you expect it to stop and how can you complain. Go to jury duty, demand to be on jury duty, and vote.

Black men, take your place. Raise these children and be a solid example. A child needs love, support, and guidance. Black women, make sure you allow men to have a relationshiop with his child. If it does not work out between the two of you; do not punish the child. If you have a father that is ready, willing, and able to be in his child's life, make it happen.

Get in it to stay in it. While it is true that all relationships will not work; black people must continue to value and respect the institution of the marriage union. This is critical. Marriage requires work, discipline, and commitment.

African Americans are correct that they deserve the rights and attention of the country as they earned full citizenship. Unfortunately, in practice, the black crisis is not dealt with as an American crisis. If the same numbers included white Americans, these issues would be seen as an American crisis. When black America has a dilemma, many white racists and our government are quick to point out that it is a black problem. If it were an American crisis, as it should be, since black Americans have earned their citizenry, they would fix it in short order.

An observation of American society clearly shows that non-African Americans own a majority of the businesses in the United States. African Americans only hold only a small number of businesses in the United States. Black Americans are continually dependent on white America for employment opportunities. The outcome is that black Americans do not become economically empowered. The easiest way to change this situation is for the black community to change their mentality towards business and entrepreneurship. Without a doubt, African Americans are known to be hardworking and determined; if black Americas were so lazy, why did they go to Africa to get people to do the labour. They recognized the mental toughness and physical abilities of the Africans. During slavery, black Americans did most of the building and toiling, which resulted in the wealthiest nation in the world. Business ownership is necessary.

Jury reform and participation are exceptionally vital to justice in the court system. Until black advocates, activists, and leaders impose pressure to change the jury system, American black men and women will continue to be victims of this system. Ultimately, no police, politician, district attorney, or prosecutor can curtail this crisis until the jury system is reformed. Black activists should set in the courtrooms and observe the juries of these black defendants and put pressure on lawmakers, courts, prosecutors, and jury commissioners to change this system. Black lives have to matter to the people on the jury panel.

Until the jury; money; vote; and pride for values, family, and self-respect comes Black, black people will continue to be pimped by their former slave masters.

BREAK THOSE CHAINS AND MAKE IT HAPPEN.

PEACE AND LOVE TO GOD (ALLAH, S.W.T.)
AND THE ANCESTORS

REFERENCES

Anderson, Claud (2001). *Powernomics: The National Plan to Empower Black America.* Powernomics Corporation of America.

Gau, J. M. (2018). *Statistics for criminology and criminal justice.* Sage Publications.

Nine Charts about Wealth Inequality in America (Updated). Apps. urban.org. (2020). Retrieved from.https;//apps.urban.org/features/wealth-inequality-charts

Seah, K. Y., Fesselmeyer, E., & Le, K. (2017). Estimating and decomposing changes in the White–Black homeownership gap from 2005 to 2011. *Urban Studies, 54*(1), 119-136.

The initiative, P. (2020). *Prison Policy Initiative.* Prisonpolicy.org. Retrieved 23 August 2020, from https;//www.prisonpolicy.org

Walker, J. T., & Maddan, S. (2019). *Statistics in criminology and criminal justice.* Jones & Bartlett Learning.

Walton, H., Puckett, S. C., & Deskins, D. R. (2012). The African American electorate: A statistical history. C.Q. Press.